Commun e sumption

Reflections On The Rise Of A
Digital Age

Simon Kennedy

DEDICATION

This book is dedicated to all those who have
continued to support and encourage my artistic
practice. I would particularly like to thank my ever
patient partner Elizabeth Barlow without whom I
may never have found the confidence to undertake a
great many projects to date.

CONTENTS

ACKNOWLEDGMENTS

To all the people who have inspired the thoughts and writings in this book and the accompanying exhibition.

Preface

What was the first thing you did this morning? Have a coffee? Take a shower? Brush your teeth? Or, like so many of us; did you spend those first few moments anxiously feeling for your phone or some other device, in order to check for overnight message streams and online activity? Or maybe you've left home without one of your beloved gadgets and experienced a level of panic so acute that you've actually returned home to pick it up, even if this has meant being late for work or an appointment. If this sounds like you, then rest assured you're not alone but how many of us pause to question this excessively, neurotic behaviour that is now considered the norm?

As a visual artist it is my job to notice things, to sit in silent observation whilst people go about their business. It's a bit like being a spy but devoid of all the fun stuff, the high octane car chases and adrenalin fuelled

1

shoot-outs. If there's a pay off to be had (which I think there is) it comes much later, when your mind has been to work on all manner of data and has somehow reconstituted it into a beautifully succinct and creative gesture. Just as an author yearns to pen the next best-seller or a director a box office hit, the artist wishes to (at least once in their lifetime) create a piece of work that transcends race, gender, religion or culture in favour of something we can all get our heads around, a truly universal expression; something akin to a smile perhaps.

About five years ago in my role as artist/spy, I assigned myself the task of observing something that has been edging its way into almost every aspect of modern life, so much so in fact, that any quality of 'otherness' it may have once possessed has since disintegrated and that 'something' we now refer to as *Digital Culture*. From purchasing my first (rather chunky) mobile phone to typing those first tentative letters of an E. Mail, I sensed that something was changing but I had no idea back then just how all encompassing or significant this change was going to be.

As an artist, I felt duty bound to say or rather make something about it and to that end "Commun -e Sumption" (the exhibition) was conceived. The term itself was created by blending a number of words that referred to what I felt at the time, were key elements of so-called digital culture; *Communication, Community, Electronic, Consumer and Consumption.* As with most creative processes, prior to getting my hands dirty and making actual work(s), It was necessary to carry out some research that would act not only as a catalyst for ideas but also provide something of a back story for the artwork(s) and general flavour of the exhibition. In the meantime, small articles and even news reports were sporadically popping up (albeit quite tentatively) airing various concerns related to the new digital age, such as; How is constant digital distraction affecting our attention?

How has the internet altered the way in which we educate not only ourselves but also our children? Is first hand (in the flesh) experience playing second fiddle to secondary experience, mediated by digital devices?

For me this was quite exciting because when I first began to think about digitisation and its wider implications, very little was actually being said about it, at least not in the public domain. My own thoughts and ideas no longer felt like those of an overly cautious parent or naysayer but were legitimised by the fact that numerous studies and research were being carried out by specialists in the field, looking in great detail at a number of issues touched upon by 'Commun -e Sumption'. Being an artist involved in creating works for a specific show, commenting on specific themes, had furnished me with an excuse to do a bit of digging, to scratch beneath the increasingly shiny and reflective surface of digital culture but without this excuse, I myself would probably be non the wiser and would have continued to be swept (unquestioningly) along with the virtual current.

'Commun -e Sumption' *the book,* serves two purposes. On the one hand it provides a back-story for the works themselves and aims to shed some light on what inspired them and how they came into being. A widely understood model of 'what art is' and what 'artists do' has ceased to exist. Most of us if we watch the news or read the papers are aware that it is no longer solely concerned with the traditional strands of painting, drawing and sculpture but without any kind of formal arts training or knowledge of art history, how is the average Joe to make sense of what people like me shove in front of them? The leap between what is going on in the artists head and what they present as the end result I.e. the artwork, can sometimes be huge (even for the artist). It's assumed that the odd paragraph of interpretation accompanying the work; acts as a footbridge between 'viewers eyes' and 'artists head' but all too often the footbridge itself is more akin to *The Temple Of Doom;*

fully equipped with booby-traps
and un-crackable cyphers. Just as
in a film each character has his
or her own back-story adding
weight and substance their
persona, the same is true of a
work of art. Being privy to the
stuff in the background or context
if you prefer, can help us to
understand what has been put in
front of us and why.

'Commun -e Sumption' (the
book) can also be read in its own
right by anybody who may be
interested in the far reaching
effects of new media technologies
in relation to our social,
psychological and physical lives.
In other words, it is by no means
imperative that you've seen the
exhibition in order to make sense
of what's written here. This
publication does not constitute an
in depth analysis of particular
artworks but rather it presents a
combination of research, spattered
with a generous helping of my own
thoughts and observations on the
various themes and issues that
have inspired me along the way.
What's contained within these
pages does not attempt to draw
airtight conclusions in respect

of

new media and how it may or may not be affecting us.

Given the shear speed and scale at which digital technologies are progressing, what seems like a pertinent issue today, could well be irrelevant tomorrow. 'Commun -e Sumption' merely offers food for thought from the angle of a creative as opposed to academic soul. Being an artist affords me the luxury of distance. To sit outside of the mob, to deliberate, to ponder, to formulate new ideas, new ways of looking. This all sounds very passive and *laissez-faire* but I suspect that for many artists (not just visual) a great deal of activity takes place in your head long before the pen touches paper or brush flows on canvas. I would like nothing more than to re-affirm the romantic notion of artists idly throwing paint around in some *shabby chic* garret, existing on little more than wine , cheese and a hedonistic lust for life but appealing a picture as this paints , it is no more realistic than the image of a writer who casually saunters through life articulated by fleeting affairs and sipping coffee in trendy Parisian cafés...

The visual arts affords the viewer a moment of pause, an opportunity to re-group, to reassess their own stance in relation to what's put in front of them. In a consumer driven society we are treated more and more like a herd of anaesthetised animals every day. We are told what to eat, where to eat, what to wear, what not to wear, how to communicate, how to work and play, which way to vote, which Gods to idolise and ultimately how to live and how to die. It's easy to see how amidst this constant barrage of poking and prodding we become resigned to the role of passively consuming (often without question), anything and everything that is put under our noses. If 'Commun -e Sumption' does little else than to re-ignite a natural tendency towards curiosity, question and debate, whilst at the same time inspiring us to be a little more mindful of the hold that 'digital culture' has on us, then I have (at least in some small way) achieved a well meant goal. If, as defenders of the subject will often postulate *'It is simply a tool',* then we should not feel bullied or forced; either, into a reliance or dependency so great, that the symptoms of abstaining are alarmingly similar to those of a patient suffering from substance abuse, or into feeling that we should employ it for every conceivable task irrespective of suitability or the chance of an agreeable outcome...

1 Age Of Distraction

Growing up in a quaint but quiet village, I often recall the excitement felt by my sister and I, when our Mother used to take us once a week to visit the City of Chester. Strangely enough, it's not so much the place that sticks in my mind but rather the journey. After my Father passed away our Mother had given up driving, so instead we would take the bus. All things considered the journey probably took about forty-five minutes which to a child of nine or ten years old can feel like an age. But it didn't. From the moment we left the bus stop to arriving at our destination, mum would be pointing things out and engaging with us in a way that is rarely seen nowadays. A combine harvester slowly gnawing its way through a field of crops, a flashy looking sports car, a group of workmen assessing a pothole in the road, nothing was too mundane or inconsequential to comment upon. As people were picked up along the way she would say hello and enter into casual chit chat with people she knew and even people she didn't. The best part was when somebody made her laugh. She had the kind of laugh that would cut through any other noise within a two mile radius. The more she tried to stop herself the worse she would be. Her face used to turn so red I sometimes thought she might burst! This in turn would set me and my sister off giggling uncontrollably. What made these trips so enjoyable was that our Mother didn't just view the journey as a means to an end, but as part of the whole experience.

Distraction As The Norm

How different this scene would look today. Despite the obvious nostalgia infused in such a recollection; 'something is different' and I mean 'really different'. In the same scene today my sister and I would both be staring 'bog-eyed' at shiny screens, scrolling and wiping our way through that forty-five minute journey, with earphones firmly supplanted, even if our mother wanted to get our attention (which she wouldn't because she too would be checking for updates and message streams on her own device) it would seem like a gross inconvenience.

Having never learnt to drive I myself still rely on all manner of public transport to get about and it doesn't seem to matter what form it takes; plane, train, bus or boat the view is always the same. A sea of lowered heads, eyes transfixed as if in an 'otherworldly trance' and hands fervently tapping, typing and scrolling. Rather than conversation the only thing audible is an electronic, jazz like discord of message alerts and ringtones. I used to find the phenomenon so curious that I would amuse myself by playing a game whereby, I would count in my head how long it was before individual passengers proceeded to getting out some sort of electronic device. Much to my dismay, even this has been thwarted by our insatiable appetite for constant distraction, since nowadays people are glued to their chosen devices before they even sit down!

I knew I had to make a piece of artwork that somehow commented on this behaviour. I would occasionally try to bring it up in conversation but quickly realised that people weren't yet ready to critique their own behaviour and were very defensive about their new toys. They were just too close and far too busy playing to see themselves or their behaviour from an observers point of view. I even questioned myself, wondering if I was seeing what I wanted to see, maybe my own view was exaggerated by a cautionary disposition in the face of anything new.

I did manage to have one conversation though, albeit with my partners 15 year old son about this phenomenon. Born in the late nineties, he's been brought up knowing little else and is a perfect example of the so-called 'digital-native'. At first he claimed to see no difference between today's digital devices and the somewhat clunky 'walk-mans' and C.D players of the late eighties - early nineties. To an extent I agreed with him, it's true that every generation has it's own minor and major advancements but surely not all of them could be seen to be key components attributing to a major cultural shift. I suppose its perfectly plausible to suggest that the 'personal stereo' was in fact a precursor to the iPod generation. But that doesn't necessarily make it the same. One fundamental differences is that the 'Walkman'(at least the early ones) had a single function; to play music, so unless you actually wanted to listen to music, there was no reason (other than fashion) to have your device out or on your person. It's worth pointing out here that just listening to music is no more distracting than just writing a letter. The difference is when I'm trying to write a letter but my phone is alerting me to all manner of updates, drawing my attention away from the task at hand. "Distraction is when my attention is hampered or drawn away from something I'm already doing."

Unlike today's digital technology which was initially

aimed at the professional adult but has since been hijacked by youth culture, (the earliest probably being the pager) the 'Walkman' was aimed and marketed at the younger demographic as a symbol of freedom and portability. In other words 'you would rarely have witnessed entire families, each with their own 'Walkman' simultaneously listening to music'. The 'walkman' was a symbol of youth, teenage rebellion and counter culture. If too many oldies like me had used them, kids would have dropped them like hot cakes. But Perhaps the most obvious difference is that you couldn't live your life through your 'Walkman' in the way that we now live our lives through our smart-phones and tablets. "There was no element of connectivity". I couldn't buy things with my 'Walkman', I couldn't check my bank balance or contact a friend. I couldn't shout (tweet) my disapproval of Government policy, I couldn't watch a film or create a document, I couldn't post pictures or have it locate my position on a map. This may or may not prove to be a positive resume, only time will tell, but what is clear is "that our current devices have gone far beyond being mere tools for making life easier, the distinction between them and our life is no longer discernible". My partners son begrudgingly admitted that maybe there was a difference between today's devices and those of my generation. But that wasn't the end of it, with regards to the multifunctional aspect, he asked me; "if a book could also play a film, or music, or turn into a camera, why wouldn't you want that?" The conversation continues...

At work or in public we are increasingly subjected to an ever

changing myriad of distractions. Both the real and the virtual

worlds are fast becoming jungles of 'hyper-links' where every distraction is surrounded by or pointing to multiple enticements and other distractions. If you visit any major City you'll realise that this kind of bombardment is nothing new. Advertising reigns supreme in modern society, occupying public spaces and ultimately invading the private sphere of people. Public

space has long since been a
gigantic billboard for products of
all kinds. This hasn't gone
unnoticed (no pun intended) or
without criticism. Kalle Lasn, co
founder of *Adbusters* and one of
the most outspoken critics of
advertising, considers advertising
to be *"the most prevalent and
toxic of all the mental
pollutants"* (8). Christopher
Lache, American historian and
social critic, states that
advertising leads to an overall
increase in consumption in
society; *"Advertising serves not
so much to promote products as to
promote consumption as a way of
life"* (8). That said, we can at
least escape the sensory overload
of 'out there' by retiring to the
so-called privacy of our own homes
(provided we don't turn on the
television or radio, or pick up a
magazine...). Nice try, the
'mobilization' of our beloved
gadgets and gizmo's ensures that
there is quite literally no escape
from incessant distraction, put
simply *"Where we go – they go"*.

When, on the odd occasion I
have plucked up the courage to
voice my concerns in regard to

what I have decided to refer to as *"digital Zombification"* I'm quickly shot down with such standardised responses as *"get with the times"*, *"you're technophobic"* or *"it's progress, this is the future"*. I'll be the first to admit that I'm no 'computer geek' and I do approach new technologies with the same degree of suspicion as I would any other consumer bandwagon I'm invited to hop on. But if this level of interruption and distraction really is the future, then shouldn't we be a little more concerned with the long term social, biological and psychological effects?

Cause For Concern?

In a bid to test my own sanity and to further inform any ideas for artworks on this subject, I set about researching the notion of 'digital distraction'. As it turned out, I was not alone. Whilst there has been no definitive medical or scientific evidence to prove *without doubt* that the use of digital technologies have a detrimental effect on us, there has been a number of studies pointing in that direction.

Without attention, how can learning take place? If I want to know how to do something, I must be capable of paying attention for at least as long as it takes a teacher or master to instruct me. If I want to write a competent book review, I need to remember (if only loosely) what took place between the pages, If I haven't been paying attention my review is likely to be substandard. Amidst the unrelenting circus of distraction that digital culture insists we attend, how is a child's brain or even an adult brain for that matter, expected to stay focused or pay attention to anything for an extended period of time?

According to two recent surveys; "there is a wide spread

belief among teachers that students constant exposure and use of digital technology is adversely hampering their attention spans and ability to persevere in the

face of challenging facts".
Researchers are of course keen to
note that the findings represent
subjective views of teachers and
should not be seen as definitive
proof that this kind of technology
affects students capability to
focus. That being said;
researchers who performed the
study and scholars who study
technology's impact on behaviour
and the brain, admit that the
studies are significant because of
the vantage point of teachers who
spend hours every day observing
students. One survey was conducted
by the *Pew Internet Project* *(2)* a
division of the *Pew research
centre"* that focuses on
technology related research. The
other was conducted by *"Common
Sense Media"* *(9)* (a non-profit
organisation in San Francisco
which advises parents on media use
by children). It was conducted by
Vicky Rideout, a researcher who
has previously shown that media
use among children and teens ages
8-18 has grown so fast, they on
average spend twice as much time
with screens each year as they
spend in school.

Teachers not involved in the

survey echoed the findings. Molina-Porter age 37 (an English teacher at Troy High School,

Fullerton, California) said *"I'm an entertainer. I have to do a song and dance to capture their attention"*. She teaches accelerated English to students, but has noted a marked decline in the depth and analysis of their written work. There is mounting *'indirect'* evidence to suggest that constant use of digital technology can affect behaviour, especially in younger brains, because of the heavy stimulation and rapid shifts in attention. It's interesting to note that despite the fact that roughly 75 percent of 2,462 teachers surveyed said the internet had a "mostly positive" impact on students research skills, nearly 90 percent said that digital technologies were creating *"an easily distracted generation with short attention spans" (2)*. Of the 685 teachers surveyed in the *"Common Sense Project" (9)* 71 percent said they thought technology was hurting attention span "somewhat" or "a lot". 60 percent said it hindered students ability to write and to communicate face-to-face, and almost half said it hurt critical thinking and ability to do homework. Dr Dimitri Christakis, who studies the impact of technology on the brain said heavy technology use *"makes reality by comparison un-interesting"*.

During interviews a number of teachers worryingly described what might be called "Wikipedia Problem". Which basically means that students have grown so accustomed to quick answers with just a few keystrokes, that they are more likely to give up when an easy answer eludes them. Having observed my own 15yr old son racing at break-neck speed through his homework assignments, this is certainly something I can vouch for. As a research tool the internet is undoubtedly useful but due to the colossal amount of information, articles, blogs and posts on any given subject, it can also be rather overwhelming and daunting, even for an adult. It makes sense that given the environment, schools want our children to be computer literate and competent at using 'the tools of the day' but the kind of focused attention necessary to sift through swathes of digitised information, is exactly (and somewhat paradoxically) the kind of attention they lack since in *'their worlds'* receiving information is instant and rarely longer than 140 characters.

In an article for the *New York Times (2)* Matt Ritchel points out that researchers say whilst the lure of these technologies affects adults too, it is particularly powerful for young people. The risk they say, is that the developing brains can become more easily habituated than adult brains to constantly switching tasks and less able to sustain attention. *"Their brains are rewarded not for staying on task but for jumping to the next thing"* said Michael Rich, an assistant professor at *Harvard Medical School* and executive director of the *Centre on Media and Child Health* in Boston.

According to the NHS, ADHD or *attention deficit/hyperactivity disorder,* is the most commonly diagnosed behavioural disorder in the UK, affecting 2-5% of school aged and young children (53). Whilst internet addiction may be a growing concern for adults, studies show that there is far greater concern for children because internet addiction can possibly lead to ADHD, hostility and social phobias. Researchers surveyed 2,293 seventh graders in Taiwan, noting that 10.8% of them developed an internet addiction over time, furthermore researchers discovered that those found to be addicted to the internet, suffered from ADHD and increased hostility.

It would be easy to label reports and articles like these as nothing more than attention grabbing headlines seeking to sow the seeds of 'digital fear'. We used to say similar things about television and how it was rotting our children's brains but such comparisons are surely naïve. The television was far from being a

personalised control centre or hub. Just like the C.D players and Walkmans, we did not live our lives through our television sets or suffer anxiety attacks when we had to leave them at home for eight hours in order to go to work. Change rarely goes uncontested and when something new is introduced in the name of progress, whether it be social, political or technological, it's positive attributes must surely be weighed against any short or long-term negative or detrimental effects. Caution is often viewed as a weakness or even cowardice, our prime-ministers, governments, heads of state and presidents would seek to inspire and strengthen our feeble hearts with talk of fearlessness in the face of threat. But just like 'fight or flight', caution serves a purpose, in the main, one that means rash or ill informed decisions don't come back and bite you in the ass. A lesson that the world's banks have learnt the hard way. Perhaps a little more caution in the first instance would have paid dividends in the long run. But when students themselves openly admit that their devices are hindering their education, is it really wise to ignore them?

In an article in *USAtoday.com* (30) Chris Blandy, aged eighteen and a senior at Cherry Hill High School West says; *"I find it sad that I get more work done at 11 or 12:30 at night because that is when everybody else is asleep"*. Mellissa Malik aged seventeen, also a student at Cherry Hill, says that cellphone distractions sometimes cause her to take twice as long to complete a homework assignment. She says; *"Something that used to take me half an hour, now takes an hour because text messages and other things can distract you"* (30).

What I've included here is only a fraction of the ongoing studies, research and reports being carried out in the name of 'digital distraction'. What we would class as 'definitive evidence' that digital technology is having a detrimental effect on us, I'm not sure. How many studies would have to show similar findings? To what extent would our children's performance in the classroom have to plummet before we took notice? How many hours a week would we have to spend online before being diagnosed as having an addiction? Scientifically, the answers to these questions are as

of yet inconclusive but is it
always necessary to wait for
science before we act? We find
ourselves in a precarious
situation. We've invested so much
time, money and energy in this
brave new 'hyper-connected' world
of ours, that we're reluctant to
question it, let alone
occasionally abstain. As with any
other kind of addiction, the first
step to recovery is admitting
there's a problem. If we continue
to bury our heads in 'virtual
sand' it will only make that
recovery more agonising and
painful. Scientists are not the
only ones bestowed with a pair of
eyes and reason. Why not have a
day off from your devices, hop on
a bus or go for a walk and just
observe how dependant we've
become. Then honestly ask yourself
is there cause for concern?

Sweet Memes

The word *meme* is a shortening of
'mimeme' in ancient greek meaning
"imitated thing". British
evolutionary biologist Richard
Dawkins, first brought this word
to prominence in his book

The Selfish Gene (1976). Most simply, a meme is an idea, behaviour or style that spreads from one person to another within a culture. A meme can be transmitted from one mind to the next in a number of ways such as writing, speech, gestures, rituals or other imitable phenomena. Could it be that when our children cuddle up to their smart phones in bed, that we are actually witnessing a meme in action?

Unlike other less ubiquitous technologies, today's portable devices see no boundaries, geographical or otherwise. Our offspring are just as distracted beyond the school gates as they are within them. If I can manage to prise my sons blackberry out of his fidgeting hands long enough to watch a family movie, then that is no small victory. But the drama soon begins again when I instruct him to leave his device downstairs at bed-time. What ensues for the next ten minutes or so, is a somewhat overly acted but nether-the-less passionate monologue, hell bent on convincing me that I am being, in his own words; 'over the top' and that it is perfectly normal for him to want to sleep with his phone. When he realises that I'm not going to budge and that he is actually too tired to sit it out, off he goes upstairs, mumbling to himself like somebody three times his age. I do agree with him on one thing though. It has become perfectly normal and to a greater or lesser extent accepted, that kids go to bed with their phones.

Little wonder then, that a poll in 2006 by the *National Sleep Foundation (27)* found that only twenty percent of adolescents get the recommended nine hours sleep and forty-five percent, less than eight hours on a school night. As it turns out, watching good old fashioned television is the most popular activity amongst teens before bed but surfing the net and instant messaging is close behind with forty four percent. I wouldn't be surprised if this figure was much greater if a poll were to be carried out today.

Of course many teenagers will claim, like my own, that they take their phones to bed because they use the alarm to get themselves up in the morning. Lol (laugh out loud), sorry I couldn't resist but how many parents have looked in on their teens at one or even two o'clock in the morning only to be greeted by an strange glow where their heads should be? Abducted by aliens? We're not that lucky. Is it as I once suspected that all our kids are secretly doctors? Maybe that's why they're on call 24/7. Joking aside this is a serious problem. Suzanne Phillips (whose a real doctor) states on her blog

This Emotional Life (28) that this 'on call' 24/7 status is largely down to obligation. Our children feel like they have to be there on the other end of some device, otherwise friends may get angry or upset if a message or phone call is not responded to immediately. This raises another issue not yet touched upon which might be worth mentioning here. It's not enough that our "new best gadgets" are constantly distracting and interrupting us, they are also making us speed obsessed when it comes to interacting with others. The most disrespect one can cause in the world of texting (and especially for teenagers) is to take longer than a split second to reply or worse still, to get distracted by something else and forget to reply at all! It doesn't matter how we reply, with a barrage of acronyms or *net-speak,* just so long as its quick. Speechless moments are simply not cool, pausing for thought alluding to cognitive deliberation and process has been done away with or as the late William Safire wrote in On Language, his New York times column: "The pregnant pause has been digitally aborted" (55). Everything must have a short-cut, emoticons, abbreviations, initial-isms and contractions all rallying together and for what? To give us more time of course, and what will we do with this time, read a book, go for a walk, cook a romantic meal for our significant other? If my teenage son is anything to go by then the answer is a resounding 'no'. Instead we utilise this saved time to instigate more exchanges of something which gets slightly further removed from language each day... and sure enough we're right back where we started.

Given that teens need about nine hours sleep compared to an adults eight, having your phone set to vibrate every time your friend posts an update or messages you, is hardly conducive.

It is highly probable that teen sleep deprivation is a contributing factor to their inability to concentrate in school, as sleep deprivation is associated with memory deficits, impaired performance and alertness. The loss of intense sleep or REM can result in many things such as increased irritability, anxiety and depression as well as reduced concentration and creativity. It's not just sleep that is affected by this constant connectivity. Growing up and being a teenager is very much about striking a balance between time with your friends and time with your family. When I was a teen, coming home from school meant spending time with my mother and sister. As much as I may have bemoaned it at the time, looking back I wouldn't trade it in. In the shadow of today's technologies, our children's constant connection with their peers, makes the separate parental and family domain obsolete. This could in many ways hurt their self-development with regards to self-esteem and formulating identity.

It seems that 'digital distraction' and our appetite for it knows no boundaries. Awake or asleep it is ever present, lurking and waiting in the silent interludes that continue to get smaller and smaller, but the really scary part is "so are we".

The Efficiency Paradox

Writing for the *Wall street Journal* (1) Rachel Silverman points out that in the time it takes to read her article most of us would have paused to check our phone, answer a text, switched to desktop to read an e-mail from the boss or glanced at Facebook or Twitter

messages popping up in the corner our screens. Distraction in the workplace is nothing new but the modern workday Silverman claims is custom-built to destroy individual focus. Open plan offices and an emphasis on collaborative work, leaves workers with little insulation from colleagues chatter. Ceaseless meetings and internal e-mails means that workers increasingly scramble to get their "real work" done in the margins, either early in the morning or late in the evening. In addition, the tempting lure of social-networking streams and status updates makes it all too easy for workers to interrupt themselves. Studies have found that office workers are interrupted or self-interrupt roughly every three minutes. Once thrown off track, it can take up to 23 minutes for a worker to return to the original task says Gloria Mark, a professor of *informatics* at the University of California, Irvine, who studies digital distraction *(1)*.

The vast majority of us would not like to admit that our 'digital vices' or new-found state of anxiously, anticipating the next distraction, is a problem. I think partly because every e-mail, message alert and notification, releases within us a 'miniature high', a hit of 'self - validation'. "Someone has messaged me - therefore I matter". (This isn't as crazy as it sounds because remarkably neuro-imaging has recently shown that texting back and forth for example, floods the pleasure centres of the brain, the very same area that lights up when using heroin). But if the problem doesn't exist , then why are businesses

worldwide introducing new protocols and pilot schemes in a bid to drastically lessen 'workplace-distraction'? In another article for the *Wall Street Journal (12)* Rachel Silverman tells us that "Companies are going to great lengths to reduce digital distraction in order to help employees stay focused". Research group *Basex,* estimated that information overload and resulting distraction led to $1 trillion in lost productivity in 2010. The data accounted for time spent managing e-mails and other content and the recovery time once a worker has become sidetracked. *Atos* a global IT service provider based outside

Paris with 74,000 employees is doing its best to phase out all internal e-mails *(13)*. German Auto Manufacturer *Daimler AG*, is trying to get employees to disconnect when they're not at work *(13)*. *Microsoft* which is responsible for creating much of the software which allows for instant interruptions is now looking for ways to create software that can be more adept at preventing unnecessary distractions *(14)*. The marketing department at *Veritas Software* have gone as far as introducing 'E-mail free Fridays' for its marketing department *(14)*. A number of businesses have even taking to banning mobile phone devices since 41 percent of workers

(according to a survey conducted by harmon.ie), remained glued to their devices during face-to-face meetings, this figure rose to 70 percent during viral meetings and webcasts *(15)*. Other such measures that businesses have been forced to adopt includes blocking access to websites deemed inappropriate or irrelevant to complete tasks and also blocking Facebook and other popular social-networking sites.

An article in the *Daily Telegraph (11)* by Carl Wilkinson entitled: "Shutting out a world of digital distraction" talks about Freedom© and Self Control©. These are computer applications that can be down loaded and configured to "increase productivity" by blocking access to the internet. In the same article neuroscientist Baroness Susan Greenfield, Professor of pharmacology at *Oxford University* asks "How can people not think this is changing your brain?" "How can you seriously think that people who work like this are the same as 20 or 30 years ago? Whether it's better or worse is another issue but clearly there is a sea change going on and one that we need to evaluate". She goes on to say "We know that all brains in the animal kingdom adapt to their environment", but "Human brains do it superlatively. It follows that if you put the brain in an unprecedented environment it will follow its evolutionary mandate and adapt. I'm a baby boomer, not part of the digital-native generation, and even I find it hard to read a full news story now. These are trends I find concerning".

It's an ironic sign of the times that, the very technology charged with making our lives easier, faster and more efficient, has the flip-side of doing the exact opposite. It seems logical that the more connected we are, the more accessible we are. The constant barrage of ads, banners, e-mails and updates has left our attention fractured and scarred upon the field of battle. We make one click forward and then several to the side, top and bottom. Travelling from a to b in a motor vehicle, may be more efficient than walking but not if I decide to stop at every burger joint, book-store or shopping complex along the way. In our physical lives we seem perfectly capable and adept at going from here to there without succumbing to the many distractions all vying for our attention. I don't know what it is about being online that makes us feel duty bound to respond to the slightest of stimulus. Maybe it's the shear transparency of the medium. Every time we log on, there's a sense that everybody else knows we're online. Chances are, 'they do'. The architecture of the online world is reminiscent of Jeremy Bentham's imagined "panopticon" or "inspection-House" a circular building of small rooms, each transparent and fully connected, in which individuals could be watched over by an all seeing inspector (10). So here we are, all alone on a constantly visible stage, what are we to do if not perform? Maybe as Dr Elias Aboujaoade suggests in his recent publication *Virtually you (29),* we all have online or 'E-personalities' that we're compelled to maintain and uphold.

Seeming to be available and capable of responding in a heart beat to the latest internal E-mail, friends request, twitter trend or status update, is all part and parcel of the super efficient, dynamic and more gregarious 'online you'. But unlike our physical lives our digital counter-parts are never exhausted, don't need to take a time-out and are always switched 'on' even when we're not. Our technology doesn't posses a conscience or display social etiquette. It doesn't care if we're at work, attending a funeral or otherwise engaged in a pursuit where its presence would be inappropriate. Like a new born child, it cries and we come running. We would like to assert that 'technology works for us' after all we created it didn't we? But the distinction between who exactly is working for who, is increasingly blurred as our technology would seem to be demanding more and more of 'us'.

Relationships Plugged In

We half expect our children to throw themselves wholeheartedly at the next new thing with little or no caution at all. But what about us...the parents, adults and guardians? Surely we demonstrate a degree of maturity and temperance when it comes to such technological fads and trends? Apparently not. Julie Scelfo wrote an article for the *New York Times* entitled: "Parenting Whilst Plugged In" *(3)*. Scelfo describes an incident whereby Janice Im (who works in early childhood development) was waiting for an elevator at the *Fair Oaks Mall* near her home in Virginia. The boy who Ms Im estimates was about 2 ½ years old, made repeated attempts to talk to his Mother but she refused to look up from her Blackberry. The child was saying "mama?, mama?, mama?" Then he starts tapping her leg. She responds by saying; "just wait a second, just wait a second". In the end the child was so frustrated that he tried to bite her leg!

Unlike other advancements such as the motor vehicle, there are no age restrictions on smart phones, blackberries or tablets except for the ones we seem so hopelessly in - adept to put in place ourselves. It's essentially 'ageless' so parents are using the same technology - and its effect on their offspring is now becoming a growing concern to some child development researchers. Sherry Turkle, *director of the Massachusetts institute of technology and self,* has been studying how parental use of technology affects children and young adults. After 5 years and

300 interviews, she found that feelings of hurt, jealousy and competition are widespread. Turkle said "over and over, kids raised the same three examples of feeling hurt and not wanting to show it when their Mother or Father would be on their devices instead of paying attention to them : at meals , during pickup after either school or an extra-curricular activity, and during sports events".

Multi billionaire Reid Hoffman founder of *LinkedIn* and one of Silicon valley's most prodigious progenitor's of online networks, insists in a debate with Andrew keen (Author of *The Cult of the amateur: How today's internet is killing our culture*) *(10)* that "the shift from a society built upon atoms to one built upon bytes, would make us more connected and thus more socially united as human beings". I wonder if the child of which Ms Im speaks, trying in earnest to 'connect' with his mother would agree?

It's not just the kids that

are playing second fiddle to the seductive glow of our smart-phones and ipads. In Facebook terms I'm still wet behind the ears, having only signed up in July 2012.

I held out for as long as I could but in the end I buckled under the weight of peer pressure on the one hand and practicality on the other. Attending 'Private views' is part and parcel of being an artist, a great place to, dare I say it 'network' and chew the fat with like minded individuals. But when it got to the point where contact details are exchanged, instead of a phone number or e-mail address, I would be instructed to 'Facebook' the interested party. Why this was seen as a more constructive route to fostering some kind of professional relationship over and above actually speaking on a phone or meeting up in person, I don't know. So here I am again, forced to mumble under my breath for fear of mass ridicule, that I didn't actually have a Facebook account - and divulging this little nugget of information generally resulted in a look that I can best describe as lying somewhere between pity and disgust. Needless to say that 'interested parties' appeared slightly 'less interested' upon receipt of this information.

I'd speculated about how social-networking sites such as Facebook could have a negative affect on relationships prior to July 2012, but as my partner soberly pointed out, *"I could hardly criticise it without experiencing it first-hand"*. So there I a was with what those on the other side of the Atlantic might call a *free-pass*. But I wasn't about to attend a *frat party* fuelled by alcohol, casual sex and smoking pot. The drug with which I was about to experiment, demanded only that I sit, type and scroll. Sending those first few friends requests and anticipating subsequent confirmations, it was easy to see how distracting and even addictive playing with all these 'pseudo lives' could be. How five minutes becomes an hour and one hour becomes three... I could see how easily I may feel justified in substituting electronic relationships for physical ones. In those first few weeks of signing up and constantly checking for messages, friends requests and updates, I witnessed first-hand how technology has the capacity to seduce and control us by pandering to our deep seated insecurity's and vulnerability.

My partner and I generally use Facebook as platform and marketing device for our projects and exhibitions but there has certainly been occasions when the dis-tractive and all consuming nature of Facebook has been an issue. But we're by no means unique, in an article on *Katu.com* (24) a guy who wishes to be known only as Randy says *"Facebook without a doubt, played a big part in the end of my marriage"*. Randy had been married for twenty

years but his wife's addiction to Facebook and online flirting, ultimately led to her having an extra-marital affair. Posting on *answers.yahoo.com* (25) James says that his wife spends more time on Facebook than she does with him. Even the kids are told to take a hike if she's chatting online.

Whilst again, there is no empirical evidence to suggest that social-networking sites such as Facebook have led to an increase in divorce rates there is certainly anecdotal evidence which points to the fact that Facebook is increasingly blamed as a reason for, or as evidence when filing for divorce. In 2011, 33 percent of 'behaviour petitions' contained the name of a social network, this is a big increase from 2009 when the figure was only 20 percent.

Filing for divorce on the grounds of over-using a social-networking site, is a bit like filing for divorce because my spouse watches too much television, the only difference being that my significant other cannot enter into some form of dialogue with his or her celebrity crush, merely by watching a screen. Movies are made by professionals and then get shown, the audience don't get to decide who should get with who, or who should be gunned down in blazes of glory and who should survive. In this sense, regardless of a film being a sequence of moving pictures, the viewer is essentially 'passive'. In contrast, Facebook is the biggest movie collaboration of all time with a cast of millions. We can switch characters whenever we like and write the script as we go along. But most significantly Facebook is 'active', we get out what we put in. If I don't post for weeks on end then my page remains dormant with little or no activity.

Social-networking sites may well provide us with the stage, but we are far from seasoned professionals. We're amateurs caught in the mesmerising glare of our own names and profile pictures, not yet capable of a restrained or economic performance. The tragic irony is that we spend so much time supposedly communicating that we neglect those closest to us who really need and would appreciate our undivided attention.

Studies such as these in addition to my own experiences and observations have inspired a number of artworks under the "Communi-sumption - Age Of Distraction banner". The use of text in the form of the written word has often a played a major role in my artworks, due to its inherent power and persuasiveness. "RED-ALERT" (2013) and "A DISTRACTION IN RED AND GREEN ON THE LEFT" (2013) allude to the myriad of distractions we've become accustomed to on a daily basis. Banners, ads, spam and message alerts of all kinds are increasingly more invasive and their rhetoric more vociferous. What became apparent observing this brand of distraction, was that the sense of urgency they espoused was often grossly out of context with the message. Another as of yet untitled work in this series, takes shape in the form of a text-based animation. We are initially confronted with an empty screen which slowly begins to fill with the kind of alerts and interruptions we're exposed to, at home, at work or at play. Each alert has its own accompanying sound and as the density of alerts increases, so too does the digital cacophony of noise. By the time the animation has finished the bright yellow background is barely visible through the thick fog of black text. This is not a pleasant piece of work, it's not meant to be, but it does go some way in highlighting the veracity and unforgiving nature of 'digital distraction'. Very often we don't see things clearly or for what they actually are, unless we isolate them and put them under the microscope so to speak. Scientists do this all the time and so do artists, the studio is just as much a laboratory as anything else. By isolating, mimicking and monumentalising the kind of distractions which are now commonplace, these works invite the viewer to 'really' question the nature, significance and validity of such constant interruption.

2 The Atrophy Of Experience

On a surprisingly sunny day in March 2012, my partner and I were in Manchester, working on a new art project that involved minor interventions in public spaces. We knew it was around the time of the Queens diamond jubilee but hadn't realised she was actually due to visit Manchester on that same day and would be having lunch at the Town Hall. After that she was scheduled to unveil the 'Jubilee Garden' in Albert Square, the exact same square that we were setting up our interventions.

For us, this was quite fortuitous as it guaranteed there would be a substantial public presence that would hopefully engage with our work (which was now under a great deal of scrutiny from security services, given the occasion). As it turned out, the most we could actually do without being considered some kind of terrorist threat, was to lay out a pre-drawn 'Hop-scotch' template on the square floor.

A crowd slowly started to gather with people casually loitering and sipping take-away coffee's outside the Town Hall. Our minor intervention was viewed equally with curiosity and suspicion. Only the very young or the very old threw caution to the wind and actually had a go. But it's not really our intervention that stuck in my mind that day, I was much more interested in the unfolding behaviour of the gathering crowd. By the time the Queen was due to make an appearance, there must have been several hundred people all vying for the best vantage point to catch a glimpse of our sovereign Mother as she exited the building. There was an increased amount of chatter and the air was thick with anticipation, I felt like I a teenager at a pop concert waiting for the headline act. One by one people began to raise their arms - holding up their mobile phones and pointing them roughly in the direction of the town hall doors. Word had obviously got out that the Queens appearance was imminent. All that could now be seen was a sea of raised arms, the bodies attached straining and contorting to see what was visible through the tiny screens on the end of their outstretched arms.

I Record Therefore I am

A sociologist would have had a field day witnessing this 'herd mentality', it was as if the crowd itself was 'paparazzi' employed by the tabloids and charged with bringing back pictures for tomorrows news. When the Queen finally emerged there was a barrage of cheers. She officially unveiled the 'Jubilee Garden', made a short speech and then proceeded around the square shaking hands and exchanging niceties with the crowd. As she moved, so did the sea of arms, hell bent on recording the whole affair.

What struck me about this unfolding drama was how digital technologies have facilitated, encouraged and spawned a nation of voyeurs. As a consequence we feel the need to validate even the most mundane of our experiences either as a still image or as a moving picture. As an artist, I'm a voyeur by necessity but I've always been acutely aware that there's a price to pay for always lurking in the shadows.

Let's say I wanted to observe the behaviour(s) of people in a rally or protest march. I can either decide to infiltrate the march and become a part of it myself (in which case I risk getting physically and emotionally caught up in it) or, I can distance myself and observe from the peripheries where my observations are more likely to be objective. "To really observe something there has to be a certain amount of distance (emotional, physical or both) between the observer and the object of observation". The price I pay as an artist is that "In being so habituated to observing, I find it extremely difficult to actively participate in - or experience life events". This isn't to say that there is an obvious or definitive distinction between observation and experience, things are never quite that simple. If you watch a movie for example, part of the experience is in observing what is going on - otherwise you'd be lost. But the magic of film (or at least a good one) is that we get so enthralled in it, that we actually forget we're outside of it, sat at home scoffing cheesy puffs on the sofa. The 'experiential' element of a movie, is how it makes us feel. If you watch a horror you feel scared, if you watch a thriller you feel intrigued and if you watch a romantic film you feel mushy. But it's only by observing each frame in a particular sequence (and of course listening to the dialogue) that allows us to come way from the movie feeling like we've actually experienced something tangible.

On that sunny day in March, a crowd of several hundred people chose to forsake what I would call a 'primary - experience' for a 'secondary - experience' mediated by digital devices. I should probably explain what I mean by this terminology. When I speak of 'Primary — experience' I'm really referring to when we witness or experience something first-hand. I'm sure we've all had occasion to listen to a friend, family member or colleague, recounting some horrific or unbelievable event. They may say something like "It's true, honestly. I was there, I witnessed it first-hand". Put another way; somebody could give me the most detailed description of how a particular piece of fruit tastes. But their description is not synonymous with actually eating the piece of fruit myself. Only by eating it (experiencing it first-hand) myself do I really know what it tastes like.

I'm sure there are plenty of learned individuals out there who would argue that there is no such thing as a 'Primary or un-mediated experience' given that the human brain is the biggest mediator of them all, feverishly altering, re-arranging and processing sensory data. Scientifically speaking they are of course correct but it's not necessary to delve quite so deeply here. I'm just trying to distinguish very simply between two kinds of experience. There is obviously a difference between actually attending a 'pop concert' as opposed to watching recorded footage of a 'pop concert'. The latter I would class as a 'Secondary – experience'. Why? Because my perception of the concert is limited by the perimeters of whatever device has recorded it. More often than not, I'm reduced to two senses; sight and sound. But what about the scent of perspiration infused with dry ice, pyrotechnics and warm beer? What about the physicality of thousands of people all occupying the same space, the sense of excitement and chatter as you queue to go in...? Digitisation has massively increased representation and the transference of human experience. But human experience is *'multi-modal'* because we exist on several levels simultaneously. Our sense organs are perhaps the most obvious indicator of this, we see, hear, taste, touch and act. In this regard a so-called 'primary – experience' is generally an altogether more comprehensive and complete experience, it is 'lived through' rather than observed. In contrast, a so called 'secondary-experience' is partial and incomplete, it has all the ingredients but lacks the seasoning.

Of the hundreds of people who saw the Queen that day, I wonder how many of them could recall any subtleties or nuances of the occasion? All that really seemed to matter was to record the whole affair as if doing so would somehow make it more valid, more real.

It's not that I'm trying to be a complete 'kill-joy', I would expect people to take a couple of snaps of less prominent celebrities than the Queen, but record the whole event as if your life depended on it? It's about now that hardcore defenders of tech will be jumping up and down saying "What about cam-corders and digital cameras?" For those of you old enough to remember them, you'll also recall that they were quite big and bulky, hardly the slim-line, slithers of technology we're familiar with today. Once the initial novelty factor had worn off, they were generally reserved for pre-planned 'days out' or recording holiday footage for prosperity. Another difference that we probably took for granted was gender. How often did you see the wife or girlfriend in control of this particular piece of kit? Chances are, not very. Statistics would seem to confirm that men tend to make most camcorder purchases, a fact that has been readily exploited by sale clerks, manufacturers and advertising agencies (22). Whilst I haven't come across any hard evidence to suggest that women have played a more active role in adopting the 'small, fit nicely into your handbag' sized digital camera, I wouldn't be at all surprised if this was the case. My own

observations have led me to
believe that given the means,
women are generally more prolific
'recorders of things' than men. I
think this is due in part to
women being more socially at ease
than their male counter-parts,
combined with the fact that
historically; the female of the
species are gatherers which in
modern society is probably
expressed as a yearning to
collect. When I attend social
occasions with my own family, it
is almost always one of the
females that instigate a barrage
(of what are for myself unbearably
awkward) group photo's.
In contrast, current devices are
far less 'gender' or 'age
specific'. The gender differences
that do exist are related to the
usage of the device rather than
purchasing bias, and whilst
digital cameras have certainly got
smaller, the integration of a
camera into your phone not only
eradicates the need for a separate
picture taking device but also
allows for more spontaneous photo
opportunities.

You only have to browse
Facebook, You-tube or Twitter for

a matter of seconds to see just how obsessed we've become with 'recording things'. According to research conducted in 2012 by *Nielsen Online (23)* "The most addicted users in the UK spent more than 125 hours on Facebook during the last year. This equates to more than a working week" and doesn't even include Youtube or twitter, Youtube being the second most popular social-networking site among British users. But apart from interrupting and distracting others with our incessant need to record and share everything from the painfully banal to the decidedly distasteful, what effect is this having on us?

'Digital Fire' an e-mail, marketing and digital specialist states that: "People have become alienated from events as they happen in real time. The constant urge to share – through micro-blogging sites such as twitter in particular, divides those who are experiencing and those who are documenting the event" (19). On a similar theme, I read an amusing story that made it into the National Press concerning *Janette*

Burley Hofman a Mother who had

produced an 18 point contract for her son *Gregory* to adhere to

upon receiving a brand new iphone. Three of the eighteen points that really stood out for me and would seem to echo some of the

issues raised within this chapter are as follows:

13. *Don't take a zillion pictures and videos. There is no need to document everything. Live your experiences. They will be stored in your memory for eternity.*

14. *Leave your phone at home sometimes and feel safe and secure in that decision. It is not alive or an extension of you. Learn to live without it. Be bigger and more powerful than FOMO – 'Fear Of Missing Out'.*

17. *Keep your eyes up. See the*

*world happening around you.
Stare out of the window.
Listen to the birds. Take a
walk. Talk to a stranger.
Wonder without 'googling'.*

I couldn't help but raise a slightly sorrowful smile when I read this article. The fact that a mother felt it necessary to remind her son of the importance of primary or direct experience, seemed to exemplify the all encompassing and unforgiving hold that current technology has on us.

Virtual Sculptors Of Self

I knew there was a piece of artwork in there somewhere but was having difficulty teasing it out. I was being pulled in a number of different directions, each seeming perfectly valid as avenues for further investigation. On the one hand I kept thinking about Andy Warhol. More specifically the way in which he transformed people and products into visual icons, to the point whereby the 'images' he produced were perceived to be more real than the actual physical object or person. I thought about all the profile pictures flying around in the 'virtual ether'. How they have a tendency to be semi-posed, we don't want to appear gratuitously vain but we do want to appear desirable, successful and interesting. How many of us put up profile pictures from ten or maybe even twenty years ago? How many of us could honestly say we haven't dismissed friend requests from those who choose not to have a profile picture but a default avatar of a featureless face? and I wonder how disappointed we'd be if we met a fraction of our 'so-called' friends in real life. In real life I often wake up with shopping bags under my eyes and a dribble of saliva slowly making its way down my chin. There are days when I feel so unbearably dissatisfied with my life that I'm forced to crawl back into bed to sleep it off. Despite our 'uber positive' postings and status updates that always seem to show us in a somewhat enviable light, most of us would be forced to admit that our real lives are constantly articulated by either fleeting or sustained exhaustion,

disappointment and hardship. The trouble with reality would seem to be that it's never quite 'good enough', it's not sexy enough,

not interesting enough, not cosmopolitan enough, not wealthy enough, not fast enough, not successful enough...

In the digital world, 'real time' restrictions don't apply. we are generously afforded a curtain of *'crystalline plasma'* from behind which we can project new and improved versions of ourselves. The more these new and improved 'images of self' are perpetuated by continuous posting and re-posting, the more substance they would seem acquire, to the point where we may actually find ourselves adjusting our outer or physical appearance in alignment with our virtual surrogates.

The vast majority of us have probably not had the pleasure of meeting our on-screen heroes or pop idols, just as your average Joe in the fifties would be unlikely to bump into Marilyn Monroe. Our knowledge of such people is gleaned through the world's media, PR machines and management teams that carefully filter out information and imagery suitable for mass consumption. Undoubtedly this kind of information will show their clients either in the best possible light or in a way which supports or reinforces there 'media persona'. In this sense, it really is an image that we buy into and are coerced to believe in. It's little wonder then, that stars are so indignant and irate when voyeuristic snaps of them appear in the press; taking the rubbish out, sunbathing topless, using illegal substances or having a domestic with a partner or spouse. Such occurrences go a long way in shattering the myth of their otherwise keenly edited celebrity image. This image would have us believe that these blessed individuals; never wake up with 'bed-head', perspire when its hot, say something out of turn when drunk, shout at their kids or partake in the odd bucket of junk food. Needless to say that 'real lives' cannot be controlled or airbrushed to the extent that an image can be.

Since the rise of social-networking sites and the plethora of devices facilitating our constant desire to record and document, it's not just celebrities that are purveyors of the 'cult of the image'. We too have become our own PR gurus and marketing strategist's. Indeed, we are all 'virtual sculptors', perpetually chiselling away and re-touching images of self. As we are so constantly reminded by the multi-billion dollar companies that have seduced us into sharing, 'we are all publishers now'.

As I mentioned in a previous chapter, it's a peculiar thing that most of the people we meet nowadays (if we don't already know them) would rather we 'Facebook' them about this or that, rather than meet up with our 'physical selves'. Maybe it's because some illusion will be shattered. I might annoyingly slurp my skinny latte, portray a nervous twitch when in company or have the infuriating habit of stating facts as if they were a question, and let's face it; nobody wants to deal with that. No, I would much rather make contact from behind the plasma curtain, where, if nothing else, I can at least turn you off or disengage from the conversation whenever I feel fit (usually without the courtesy of saying so). Somehow things have got reversed without us even noticing. It used to be that 'seeing' (actually not virtually) was believing but now it is more like 'seeing an image is believing' and this particular brand of seeing is synonymous with the kind of 'secondary-experience' I spoke of earlier. How many of us would suggest that an 'image' of a bus is more 'real' than an actual physical bus? Probably not that many, although I confess that I haven't actually tested this. Maybe we don't actually believe in 'images' in a scientific sense, in the same way that if we watch a fantasy film about a flying carpet we don't actually believe that carpets can fly, but suspending our belief or reason for the duration of the movie, our enjoyment of it is substantially increased. Perhaps it's all about what we've come to prefer. The world wide web is in itself an intermediary of information, both textual and visual. Given that we spend so much time within its translucent architecture, maybe its inevitable that we've come to view 'secondary-experience' either as on a par or if not somehow better and more appealing than 'primary-experience'.

I posed the question earlier; 'to be truly real is it necessary to be an image?' and the more I think about it, the more convinced I am that the answer is a resounding yes, at least in so far as, it is the the self in the form of a pre-packaged unit of information (visual and textual) that is the accepted currency of the day.

Info-Nation

I've talked a lot about so called 'images' but I don't use the word in its narrowest sense of 'a purely visual image' but more-so its wider meaning of 'a general impression presented to the public', this is the kind of image that we are forever sculpting and

re-sculpting, especially when
we're engaged in social-networking
but It's not just our carefully
selected pictures that are
involved but our likes and
dislikes, our responses to other
peoples posts, our political
stance, favourite food,
relationship status, geographical
location at any given moment...the
list is forever expanding.

This bundle of information
constitutes 'my image' and how I
would like people at large to
perceive me. Our online profiles
have evolved from being somewhat
ambiguous, sketchy outlines to
detailed and definitive 'self
portraits' (but more of a
flattering commission than a warts
and all study). The internet is no
longer a forum divulging
impersonal data, far from it. The
Internet is now a complex
organism, teeming with products
and services designed around 'the
social'. It's an immense personal
data base divulging where we are,
what we ate for breakfast, what
we're thinking, watching and
reading. Buying in to its lure, we
have become active members of a
social economy, trading in packets

of information or as cultural historian Neal Gabler says; "We have all become information narcissists" (10). We have witnessed and lived through numerous economic shifts such as hunting, agriculture and manufacturing but greater emphasis is undoubtedly, now being placed upon data. We are all living and active participants in the transition between a labour intensive economy to that of a knowledge or information led economy.

After many ours of silent reflection, it became clear that I had at least three possible options for creating artwork(s). The first was to go down the 'secondary-experience' route I discussed at the beginning of this chapter, the second, was to focus upon the construction of our 'public images' and thirdly would be to look at information as a commodity and how in recent years a purely trade based economy has been overshadowed by an economy fuelled by the exchange of information.

In an ideal world, I would

like to have made artworks that commented on all three lines of investigation. However, it's something of an occupational hazard, that artists' and creative types, irrespective of their chosen specialism, tend to have far more ideas than they could ever hope to realise. So, after much deliberation, I began to work on the idea that I could most relate to and had given a significant amount of thought. I'd been toying with the idea of a series of work(s) collectively titled: "Information Based Experiences" or IBE. The catalyst for this particular piece was actually a negative experience that my partner had recently suffered. Her Birthday was fast approaching and rather than having a big expensive celebration, she fancied just having a handful of close friends and family over for a few drinks and party games. Like most of us would do in this day and age, she invited the majority of her guests via Facebook (after all isn't this exactly the kind of thing such sites are supposed to be for?). Of course the inevitable happened, as the big day got closer, so too did the *'I would really love to but...'* messages. Understandably she felt a little deflated (who wouldn't?), it's only once a year and surely our friends could jiggle their social diaries just this once. As it happened we had a perfectly nice time anyway with close family members but the absences were seemingly made more irksome to my partner by the abundance of 'Happy Birthday' messages they found time to post on Facebook. At first I didn't really understand why this was an issue, surely receiving a message online was better than receiving no message at all. But the more I thought about it, I could empathise with how she felt. This was a perfect example of the much talked about 'flip-side' of social media that can often lead to us feeling deflated, depressed and paradoxically lonely. Just as Facebook 'likes' account for very little in the real world, the fact that we can invite our friends and acquaintances to real life events, does not translate into actual attendance. Social media may have made it easier to be electronically 'in touch' but it has also made us rather lazy as a consequence. People we would have taken the time to go and see (physically) in the past, we now contact via social media. This is a change that I think we really ignore at our own peril. Social media doesn't compare to a warm hug and a good old chin-wag over a cup of tea, especially in times of hardship such as we are experiencing at the moment. But if we're not careful we'll end up forsaking meaningful, real-life, social experiences for virtual, secondary ones, whilst at same time rearing a generation of children lacking in fundamental social skills. Rather than a last resort, social media is often used as the first point of call when we want to get in touch or speak to somebody, even when it's close friends and family. My partners son is often on Facebook conversing with his friend who literally lives next door but one!

Taking my partners 'Birthday experience' into consideration in addition to the many other observations I've already covered in this chapter, I came up with the idea of "Information Based Experiences". This work would consist of a library of small cards, with each card expounding details of a given experience. This extensive library would cover everything and anything from visiting grandma to a romantic dinner for two. Each card would display a thumbnail image of the said experience and then a step by step textual translation. Each card carries its own disclaimer in small print, stating that at no point have you physically visited grandma (for example) during this experience. This particular body of work is reminiscent of the kind of gift experiences you can purchase from a number of high street stores, the major difference being that rather than actively living through the experience, it is simply read in the same way we would read an instruction manual or profile information online.

With this piece, I really wanted the viewer to imagine a world where all of our experiences are reduced to nothing more than information or data. At first glance this may seem like a rather churlish exaggeration of the current status quo but is it really that big a leap? As the 'Grateful Dead' lyricist John perry Barlow wrote " *Coming into the virtual world we inhabit information. Indeed we become information, thought is embodied and the flesh is made word. It's weird as hell"*.

3 **Friends**

If I'm to believe my own hype
or should I say 'Facebook
profile', then I'm undoubtedly one
of the most popular people I know,
weighing in at close to nine
hundred friends! Of course by
today's standards this is a mere
drop in the virtual ocean but
having said that, I only joined
Facebook a year ago, so on average
I'm making 2.4 friends a day. Not
bad for somebody like myself who's
actually quite socially awkward to
say the least. However my new-
found 'social dynamism' was soon
put into perspective when I read
that former call girl Ashley
Dupré, who was linked in 2008 with
the then governor of New York,
Eliot Spitzer, boasted some 14,000
so-called friends. The fact that
Facebook has found it necessary
to lift its 5,000 friends limit,
indicates that our friendship
groups , circles or clouds
continue to expand at a dizzying
rate.

I used to feel quite envious
when I would over hear people on

public transport, boasting about how many friends they had accrued on social networking sites. I found myself feverishly adding up in my head how many 'true' friends I could recount and rather embarrassingly only required one hand with which to do so. But is it really possible or even practical to have so many friends? After all, friendship is ultimately a form of relationship and relationships have to be maintained, otherwise they simply dissolve or breakdown don't they? According to British anthropologist Robin Dunbar, there exists a cognitive limit to the number of people with whom we can actually maintain social relationships. This doesn't mean people we know purely by sight but relationships whereby each individual knows who the other person is and how they relate to the rest of the group. This number is proposed to lie between 100 and 230 but the commonly used value is 150 (known as Dunbar's Number)(32). This number relates to the people we actually keep social contact with and not just people that may be known to us in general. This is still quite a large number of people and maintaining meaningful contact with them all could be considered a full time job, but it's still child's play in comparison to some of the numbers being wielded around on social-media.

Primatologists tell us that due to their highly 'social' nature, primates must maintain personal contact with other members of their social group and the number of social group members a primate can track appears to be limited by the volume of the 'neocortex'(the neocortex in humans is basically the cauliflower like thing we generally associate with the brain. Ours is so big that it almost covers the rest of our older brains.) The neocortex enables much of the complex mental activity we associate with being human. It has allowed for new levels of advanced behaviour, particularly but perhaps not surprisingly 'social behaviour'. So from the point of view of a primatologist maintaining meaningful relationships with the kind of numbers prevalent in social-media, is quite simply not possible, at least not unless the neocortex were to suddenly increase quite dramatically in size and volume.

So who exactly are we kidding when we say we have 300 friends plus? I am perfectly aware that out of the 900 or so friends on my Facebook account, I personally know but a handful and even those that I know quite well, I rarely see in person. Everybody's so busy nowadays juggling family, work and of course spending huge amounts of time managing 'the virtual self'. What we have to come associate with the word 'friend' would seem to have very little in common with what is traditionally meant by that term. It is worth looking at the dictionary definition to see just how far we might have strayed.

Friend: **"A person that one likes and knows well"** and

friendship is defined as thus: **"Close relationship, companionship, intimacy, rapport, affinity, attachment, alliance, harmony, fellowship, mutual understanding, amity and comradeship"**. How many of us could honestly ascribe these kinds of qualities to the hundreds and sometimes thousands of proposed friends and friendships we profess to have? But maybe its not our fault if our modern relationships don't add up. Words are quite stoical creatures and often remain even when their original meaning or definition has long since, set sail.

The Greek philosopher; *Aristotle* proposed that the traditional idea of friendship had at least three components. 'Friends must enjoy each others company, they must be useful to one another and they must share a common commitment to the good'(34). In contemporary western society, we tend to define friendship in terms of the first component (enjoying each others company), although even this is struggling to have any kind of credence, since a vast majority of those whom we call 'friend' via social-media, have never actually been in our 'physical' company or vice versa. The second of Aristotle's components is friendship based upon utility. The shelf -life of this brand of friendship, exists only for as long as either party receives something of use or of profit. People that share this kind of so-called friendship may not even like each other. If that sounds cynical - it is, individuals who partake in this type of friendship, take pleasure in one another's company only in so far as they hope to gain advantage from it. If the advantage is removed for one party or the other, the friendship is likely to break up quickly or gradually dissolve. It's uncomfortable having to admit to such disingenuous relationships and/or motives for them but the overlapping worlds of business, commerce and politics for example, is riddled with such transactional friendships.

The third installment of Aristotle's triptych is friendship based on pleasure. Friendship between the young serves as an excellent example of this because they are so regulated by their feelings and desires. Their chief interest is their own pleasure at any given moment. As youngsters grow, their tastes change ,

which accounts for why youngsters
are so quick to make and break
friendships. Their affection
changes just as quickly as the
things that please them. The young
regularly fall in love and develop
crushes, so erotic friendship
plays a big part in this constant
shifting of affections. Erotic
friendship is of course also based
upon pleasure.

For Aristotle at least, the
most perfect example of friendship
was friendship based upon
goodness. The basic premise being,
those who desire the good of their
friends, for their friends sake.
Each loves the other for what he
is and not for any incidental
quality. The emphasis here is
undoubtedly placed upon goodness
since Aristotle posits that "what
is absolutely good is absolutely
pleasant; and these are the most
loveable qualities".

It's clear that friendship for
the ancients was anything but
universal, rather it was a rare
and precious thing that took time
intimacy and trust in order to
manifest. The rise of Christianity
undoubtedly altered the emphasis

of where and toward whom one should place their loyalty, admiration, trust and so on – and this target was of course God. The classical notion of friendship was once again revived by the renaissance. Montaigne (the french renaissance writer) wrote *"Those who venture to criticise us perform a remarkable act of friendship, for to undertake to wound and offend a man for his own good, is to have a hearty love for him"*. He avowed that his very close friendship with the humanist poet Éttiene de la boétie, stood higher not only than marriage and erotic attachment, but also than filial, fraternal and homosexual love.

Relationships in traditional societies were dominated by interest and most often would have adhered to Aristotle's "Utilitarian" model. In this sense the 'true friend' stood in opposition to the self interested "flatterer" or "false friend". I wonder how many of our so-called friends on social networks would fit into this category or particular brand of friend? Do we not find ourselves positively commenting on the posts and pictures of others in the hope that such flattery will be reciprocated?

Inevitably and for a number of reasons such as industrialization, the breakdown of the family unit, migration, displacement and the many notions attributed to modernity itself such as freedom, mobility and transience have overshadowed and all but distinguished the classical idea of friendship, a one true friend or soul-mate no longer plays a role in our culture. No more Achilles and Patriclus, Emerson and Thoreau, Goethe and Schiller or Wolf and Forster. We no longer believe that the true purpose of a friend is to summon us to the good by offering moral advice and correction. The virtuous element along with mutual improvement has been lost.

The ideals of modernity are egalitarian and all about acceptance. Our friendships have perhaps become more therapeutic than anything else, with friends taking our side, validating our feelings and generally aiding us to feel good about ourselves. We may even find ourselves defending our friends, when deep down we feel that they are in the wrong or committed a questionable action.

As the classical model has faded, new and alternative models have come to pass such as the group friendship of artists, writers, poets and musicians. These kinds of friendship circles are almost 'counter-culture' like – in setting themselves up as groups of somehow enlightened spirits, against existing structures and norms (this kind of friendship is synonymous with youth culture). Group friendship probably reached it's heights in the sixties with social forms such as the commune and the Rock'n'Roll band. These forms of friendship were celebrated and yearned for as creative places of eternal youth, sanctuaries devoid of all things adult.

With the advent of social media such as Facebook, Friendster and My-space (to name but a few), the so-called friendship circle has expanded exponentially to engulf the entire social world.

But in a world where we are quite literally "friends with everybody" in what sense are we really friends with anybody? Has the term friendship and what it represents written itself out of the picture? The same question is often asked of art, if art can be anything, then art is surely nothing...it loses it's distinction and gets lost in the sea of life.

Facebook makes our friends visible and puts them ever so neatly arranged in one place. But of course they are not really in one place and how many of these people could actually be thought of as 'real friends' is questionable. I would feel comfortable asking a real friend if they would help me move house or feed the cats whilst I'm on holiday but Could I really ask this of so-called friends gleaned through social-Media? The visual juxtaposition of friends and their image creates a mirage of emotional proximity. Is friendship dissolving before our very eyes from a meaningful relationship to a feeling...a sense of connection as opposed to

an actual one. Has friendship gone
the same way as community? Will we
find ourselves clinging to the
word, no matter how diluted its
meaning may have become? We talk
of religious communities, the
medical community and so on but
again in what sense are they
really communities. Are they not
just individuals with a shared
faith, profession or interest?
Surely to belong to a community is
to know your neighbour, to feel a
strong bond and to purposefully
club together in the interests of
the group, to have a sense of
pride etc? Gone are the days when
we would share our private
observations and experiences with
a friend. It used to be that you
could only really share such
things with one friend at a time
(on the phone, down the pub or
perhaps in person). We used to
talk and share with specific
people, people who were truly
known to us, what you said and how
you conversed would be tailored to
that specific person, their
interests, personalities and the
level of intimacy that had been
fostered between you.
We can liken this kind of sharing
of information about ourselves, to

what social psychologists would call *'self-disclosure'*. When we talk about self-disclosure, we refer to the revealing of information about oneself that others are unlikely to know about us or find out on their own. In the early days of a 'real-world' friendship, such disclosure is duly censored by each individual. If I've only met somebody a couple of times, waiting for a bus perhaps, I'm unlikely to divulge my most private or emotionally harrowing secrets. Some people we meet for the first time do in fact divulge rather more about themselves than we would care or feel comfortable to know. Our usual response to this is one of slight embarrassment and quite possibly future avoidance of said person. 'Too much too soon' can be as detrimental when it comes to friendship as 'too little too late'. In the real world, self-disclosure is gradual, starting with small snippets of information. As trust and comfort is gained we may then disclose more private and sensitive information. When we feel confident enough in a given relationship to enter into regular self-disclosure, the relationship is generally stronger as a result, so long as it is reciprocated. On-line disclosure can often let us down in this regard since there is not the same sense of obligation to 'return the favour'.

In the 'online world' we seem far less concerned about what to expose about ourselves and how much. Our in-built censorship mechanism that appears to work perfectly well in the real world, is somewhat prone to malfunction in the digital arena. Overtly sexual or provocative images, emotional breakdowns or vitriolic rants, domestic disputes with a partner or spouse, abusive or unbecoming language...

During the billions of hours that are now whiled away in front of a screen, most of us are guilty of at least one of the afore mentioned 'virtual indiscretions'. Maybe because social-media is so saturated, we think that to get noticed amidst an ever increasing totem of green dots at the side of our browsers, we must be larger than life, more provocative, opinionated or exposed than we would ever allow ourselves to be in the real world. Sometimes we share sensitive information for the benefit of a few, forgetting that others who may not be as close to us, can also view our many posts and status updates.

Nowadays we are content to just broadcasts streams of consciousness to everybody, known or not, in the vain hope that one of our many pseudo-friends will respond and in doing so validate our ever so fragile existence. We tend not to see people or individuals any more. Our friends are lumped together in one big cloud or audience of faceless bodies. The hugely successful American sitcom 'Friends' is no longer relevant, partly because our friendship groups are so huge. There just isn't enough hours in the day, week or even month to have lunch or shoot the breeze over a coffee, when we have a thousand plus friends to get through. Even if we found the time, would we really give our

undivided attention or would we be too distracted by incoming messages and maintenance of our online profiles? Close friends are 'out' and being friends with everybody is 'in'. Perhaps we try to connect with more and more people because the connection we have with existing so-called friends is ultimately unfulfilling, devoid of depth, trust , intimacy and shared experience. Have we gone for quantity over quality...thinking that this will somehow fill the void? I'm no longer required to actually know my friends, their characters, or personality traits, all that is necessary is that I know their likes and dislikes, their favorite films or books. In this sense 'Information has undoubtedly replaced experience'.

The introduction of 'electronic mail' vastly reduced the size of the letter and twitter is even more limiting. Very little of worth can be shared within these dictates and hellishly restricting perimeters. How are we to share a story or a real conversation in 140 characters? All that can really be shared is equivalent to an advertising slogan or sound-bite. The digital age would appear to be seducing us with the illusion of companionship devoid of the real life demands of a friendship. Sounds great, but surely it is in the genuine attempt to meet such demands that renders true and real friendship a worthwhile and mutually enriching experience. Posting information is fast, impersonal exhibitionism whereas telling a story takes time, patience, intimacy, subtlety and skill.

The future of friendship is as unknown as where 'digital culture' will be catapulting us next and often it is necessary to dip ones toe into the water to check the temperature. I joined Facebook a little over a year ago because I wanted to experience what all the fuss was about and to use my Facebook experience to inform my artwork. Now that I have spent a significant amount of time on the medium, I can talk about it from an experiential point of view rather than pure conjecture. In my opinion it remains an inadequate platform for attaining or fostering 'real friendships'.

There is certainly an argument for its use in maintaining contact with loved ones who may be frail, incapacitated or have migrated to far off lands. It is also fine as a marketing tool to show images of my work and inform a wider audience of what it is that I actually do (so long as I don't get too carried away with Facebook likes, which equate to very little in the real-world). In the current climate I don't suppose I could have survived much longer without some kind of online presence, it's not so much a choice any more as a necessity. Make no mistake, if there are any conscientious detractors out there choosing not to swim with the virtual masses, you will become marginalised and your life more restricted as the march to digitise 'everything' advances ever forwards.

Maybe in the future the 'Zeitgeist' appeal of social media will wane as we become increasingly disillusioned with the quality of its content and over-saturation. Perhaps we will initiate a return to more classical notions of friendship, alternatively its appeal may continue to grow but I suspect that what will make or break social-media is not attracting new customers but more-so, maintaining its billions of existing users beyond the 'honeymoon period'.

Looking at the 'friends phenomenon' has thus far spurned two pieces of work in "Communisumption the exhibition". The first is entitled: *"301 Friends In 153 Days"*. This work has taken shape in the form of a book that displays only the profile pictures of all the so-called friends I had managed to glean on Facebook in the allotted time of 153 days. As I mentioned earlier, to achieve this in real life, I would have to be making 2.4 new friends per/day. As I flick through the book, it feels like I'm flicking through the pages of a catalogue...not of clothing or home-ware but of people reduced to a singular image, carefully selected to brand themselves in the best possible way in anticipation of entering into 'the friends market'. Produced in the form of a book which can be mass produced and then sold, reinforces the idea that 'friendship' itself has been turned into a *commodity* . If this seems like an exaggeration , we should not forget that many businesses pay large amounts of money not only to buy *'Facebook friends'* but also *'likes'* and *'followers'*.

The second work I produced on a similar theme is entitled "Friends Top-Trumps". This piece of work parodies the popular children's game "Top-Trumps" but rather than dinosaurs or comic book heroes, friends of the galleries Facebook page , where *'Communi-sumption'* was first exhibited , are the subjects. The work invites the viewer to question his or her motivations when seeking friends on social-media sites. Just like the real Top-Trumps, each character displays a number of categories such as looks, associative value, hall of fame etc. Which can then be compared to the character or 'friend' of another player to see who has the highest score and will win that particular hand. Produced as a consumer item and available in packs of 40 cards , "Friends Top -Trumps" further reinforces the contemporary commodification of friendship.

Further chapters will be available soon.

Images of the Commun e sumption exhibition and further information can be found at:

www.c-sumption.blogspot.co.uk

Simon Kennedy

ABOUT THE AUTHOR

Simon Kennedy graduated from
Staffordshire University in 2004
with a first class honours degree
in fine art. Since then, Simon has
continued to build upon what is an
extremely prolific and eclectic
artistic practice. No stranger to
the written word, a great number
of the artists early works are in
fact text based and a number of
these have been published in
artist led magazine 'BLACK &
BLUE'.

World events and popular culture
have continued to influence
Simon's work as 'Commun e
Sumption' would suggest. The
artist finds the rise of new
digital technologies as
fascinating as he does perplexing,
so much so that 'Communi e
sumption' (the exhibition) focused
solely on this subject matter.

It would have been impossible to
adequately convey the artists
thoughts and rationale for this
exhibition in a single artists
statement which is how 'Commun e
sumption Chapters' came into
being. Artists will often conduct
a great deal of research that
rarely sees the light of day
beyond a sketch book or scraps of
paper stuck to a studio wall.
Since 'Commun e sumption' was
concerned with a phenomenon that
continues to affect us all and has
far reaching, social, economic and
political ramifications, the
artist felt it would not only be
useful, but at times humorous and
interesting to share at least some
of the thoughts and research that
inspired what was in the end a
visually striking, thoughtful and
engaging exhibition.

End Notes:

1.
http://online.wsj.com/article/SB100014241278873
24339204578173252223022388.html

2.
http://www.nytimes.com/2010/11/21/technology/2
1brain.html?ref=yourbrainoncomputers&_r=0

3.
http://www.nytimes.com/2010/06/10/garden/10ch
ildtech.html?ref=yourbrainoncomputers

4.
http://www.nytimes.com/2012/11/01/education/te
chnology-is-changing-how-students-learn-
teachers-say.html?pagewanted=all&_r=0

5.
http://www.nytimes.com/2010/06/10/garden/10ch
ildtech.html?pagewanted=all

6.
http://www.consumerreports.org/cro/magazine/2
012/08/phones-put-pedestrians-in-a-
fog/index.htm

7.
http://workingtitleuk.ning.com/profiles/blogs/an-
age-of-

distraction?commentId=5353999%3AComment
%3A13127&xg_source=msg_com_blogpost

8.
http://en.wikipedia.org/wiki/Criticism_of_advert
ising

9. http://www.commonsensemedia.org/

10. # Digital Vertigo, Andrew Keen (First published
in the USA by St Martins Press 2012)

11.
http://www.telegraph.co.uk/culture/books/9522845/S
hutting-out-a-world-of-digital-distraction.html

12.http://blogs.wsj.com/atwork/tag/digital-
distraction/

13.
http://hereandnow.wbur.org/2013/01/14/digital-
distractions-work

14. http://news.cnet.com/Driven-to-distraction-
by-technology/2100-1022_3-
5797028.html?tag=sas.email

15.

http://www.independent.com.mt/articles/2011-09-01/news/ict-feature-digital-distractions-297990/

16.

http://www.wired.com/magazine/2010/05/ff_nicholas_carr/

17.

http://www.thefreedictionary.com/experience

18.

 http://www.legalzoom.com/us-law/privacy/smile-youre-my-cell

19.

http://www.digitalfire.co.za/blog/how-social-media-has-affected-human-interaction/

20.
http://thenextweb.com/shareables/2012/12/31/mom-presents-18-point-contract-with-rules-of-use-to-teenage-son-would-you-be-tempted/

21.
http://www.emeraldinsight.com/rin/pdf/digital_technologies.pdf

22. http://www.videomaker.com/article/1689

23.

**http://www.telegraph.co.uk/technology/facebook/
6502237/Facebook-users-spend-three-solid-days-
a-year-on-the-site.html**

24.

http://www.katu.com/news/121864649.html

**25.
http://uk.answers.yahoo.com/question/index?qid
=20101018103316AAZyOcH**

26.

**http://www.zdnet.com/blog/facebook/facebook-
blamed-for-a-third-of-divorces-in-the-uk/6788**

27.
http://aspeneducation.crchealth.com/artic
le-teen-sleeping/

28.

http://www.pbs.org/thisemotionallife/blogs/te
ens-sleeping-cell-phones-clear-and-present-
danger

29.

Virtually you (the dangerous powers of the
E-personality) by Elias Aboujaoude

W.W. Norton & Company, Inc 2012

30.

http://www.usatoday.com/story/news/nation/
2013/01/15/students-social-media-homework-
distraction/1835461/

31.

http://www.burningthebacon.com/2009/03/05
/how-social-media-has-changed-the-
definition-of-friendship/

32.

http://en.wikipedia.org/wiki/Dunbar%27s_n
umber

33.

http://infed.org/mobi/friendship-some-
philosophical-and-sociological-themes/

34.

http://www.dailymail.co.uk/femail/article-
2256067/British-people-spend-NINE-
HOURS-day-staring-screens-time-internet-
ANY-nation-say-NetVoucherCodes.html

35.

http://www.a-
n.co.uk/publications/article/1558894/1558858

Printed in Great Britain
by Amazon.co.uk, Ltd.,
Marston Gate.